D0821921

Rave Reviews

"Everyone, from the one-pet owner to the proprietor of a grooming salon, will find this book invaluable. Veterinarians and the staff of pet hospitals, handlers and trainers, breeders and exhibitors, as well as owners and employees of pet shops, breeding and boarding kennels, and all persons connected with Poodles will deem it indispensable . . ."

—Popular Dogs

"Carefully detailed, and profusely illustrated with photographs, drawings and diagrams . . . clear and explicit instructions take the reader through the step-by-step procedures of clipping and grooming."

—Dog World

"Each step is carefully explained, down to the smallest detail, and heavily illustrated with diagrams and pictures. Although directed at Poodle owners, all dog owners can learn from the sound advice given in the bathing and grooming chapters."

—Pure-Bred Dogs American Kennel Gazette

CLIPPING AND GROOMING
YOUR POODLE
Step by Step

PEARL STONE
(OPERATOR OF N. Y. SCHOOL OF DOG GROOMING, INC.)

With an Introduction and a chapter on "Show Clips" by
JANE F. KAMP

ARCO PUBLISHING COMPANY, INC.
New York

Published by ARCO PUBLISHING COMPANY, Inc.
219 Park Avenue South, New York, N.Y. 10003

Copyright © Pearl Stone, 1965

All Rights Reserved

*No part of this book may be reproduced, by any means,
without permission in writing from the publisher, except
by a reviewer who wishes to quote brief excerpts in connection
with a review in a magazine or newspaper.*

Library of Congress Catalog Card Number 65-21201

Printed in the United States of America

ACKNOWLEDGMENTS

In addition to our students and colleagues who helped us in innumerable ways to compile this book, we are especially indebted to Roland Pletersky, photographer, Tora Shinichiro, artist and Eliane Nizet, who served as consultant.

Introduction

by
Jane F. Kamp

IT IS A PLEASURE for me to write this introduction to a book which fills a long-needed void in the world of dog grooming. The few books on the subject, which have appeared in the past, have been decidedly mediocre and inadequate.

Mrs. Stone's book is the answer to a Poodle owner's prayer. The wealth of photographs and diagrams alone are worth the price of the book, and the simple nontechnical text that accompanies the illustrations makes this a perfect do-it-yourself manual.

Poodle fanciers have long argued the origin of this unique breed. Claims have been made by England, France, Germany, and even Russia, but that question has become academic in the light of the tremendous popularity the Poodle enjoys in this country. He is undisputedly America's No. 1 breed.

The great upsurge in interest in the Poodle during the past five years is an amazing phenomenon, perhaps explainable only by historians or sociologists. Some of it is probably due to his temperament and his size; he makes a perfect house pet and is even a good apartment dweller. Of course, his overall attractiveness and jaunty manner also make him endearing. At any rate, the figures are incontestable. The Poodle has a runaway lead over all other breeds.

Mr. Arthur Frederick Jones, editor of *Pure-Bred Dogs*, official organ of the American Kennel Club, noted in 1962 that "For the third straight year the Poodle is the king in registrations. The breed has a total for 1962 of 123,865; an increase of 24,609 over 1961 and a percentage gain of 24.8%. This is a very sharp rise, one not usually made by a breed so far out in the lead, but Poodles apparently are destined to break all existing records before they reach the ceiling of their climb."

Again in 1963, Mr. Jones states: "For the fourth time in a row the Poodle is the No. 1 dog in America. Not only is it still out in front but there is no indication of its amazing popularity cresting."

Finally in 1964, Mr. Jones summarizes the whole development: "Setting a dizzy pace for all breeds is the Poodle, which moved up to an unprecedented high for any breed of 178,401 compared with 147,055 for 1963. This was an increase of 21.3%, which indicates an acceleration of its rate of increase, for in the previous yearly period it had gone ahead by only 18.7%. This sets at rest for the moment any suggestion that the Poodle's flood tide is cresting. Incidentally, the number of registered Poodles is now nearly 100,000 higher than the highest mark (78,501 in 1947) set by the Cocker Spaniel during the time it reigned for 17 years as America's No. 1 breed."

The following AKC Registration statistics show the relative standing of the five leading breeds in America. This makes the ascendency of the Poodle even more graphic.

	Poodles	German Shepherds	Beagles	Dachshunds	Chihuahuas
1960	75,291	33,701	54,170	42,727	44,600
1961	99,256	40,412	53,069	46,185	46,089
1962	123,865	44,541	47,961	44,491	45,965
1963	147,055	52,769	49,769	46,993	42,659
1964	178,401	63,163	53,353	48,569	40,966

The total number of purebred Poodles registered in the last five years with the American Kennel Club is close to 600,000, and it is estimated that the number of unregistered Poodles approximate the number of purebreds, bringing the total in the last five years alone to some 1,200,000. And there is still no sign of decline.

In view of such figures is it any wonder that dog-grooming salons are flourishing all over the country, and that breeders, veterinarians, and pet shops are adding dog-grooming departments as side lines? And is there any question as to the need for a book like this, to which both amateurs and professionals can refer?

I am proud to have collaborated with Mrs. Stone, if only on the section on "Show Clips." I have been associated with the show rings of America for the past 15 years, so I feel I can speak with authority on the subject. I also feel that I can state with some authority that the Poodle owners of America will be grateful that this long-needed work has at last been published.

J.F.K.

About the Author

For over ten years, Pearl Stone has owned and operated dog-grooming salons in California and New York. She is currently both owner and operator of the New York School of Dog Grooming. Mrs. Stone founded the school in 1963, with some hesitation and a good deal of trepidation, after receiving innumerable requests to teach dog grooming to pet owners and would-be professionals. It was an unexplored field when she began, and she ran the school on a part-time basis at first, operating a dog-grooming salon at the same time. Within a short period the school was so successful that she had to give up her dog-grooming business to operate the school full-time. Since that notable beginning, many of her students have gone on to become shop owners and excellent groomers in their own right. Their success and their many unsolicited testimonials that dot the school's walls are a great source of pride to the author.

Students watching demonstration

Foreword

THIS BOOK was born out of the need expressed by my students as well as many Poodle owners for a work that would fill the gap between the old books on dog grooming and the needs and desires of the present-day Poodle owner.

I have, therefore, undertaken to do what, to the best of my knowledge, no other book on the subject has done. To take the reader through the step-by-step process of grooming a dog, using the most up-to-date methods and equipment. For the average pet-owner it will be possible, by carefully following the procedures outlined here and by employing a little patience and practice, to keep one's own pet looking neat and trim at all times. Those with a special flair for grooming, who wish to develop into professional groomers or intend to own their own shops should plan to attend the School's Professional or Shop-Owners Courses and use this book as a handy reference.

I have selected the Poodle for demonstration and illustration in the book for a number of reasons:

1. The Poodle is the pet which requires the most frequent grooming.
2. The Poodle is the most expensive to keep well groomed.
3. Poodle patterns, or clips, are the most complex and time consuming to master.
4. The Poodle is by far the most popular breed in this country.

Other breeds, such as the Wirehaired Terrier and the Schnauzer, are relatively simple to clip. Their owners, by merely studying the basic line of this book and following the breed chart, should be able to keep them looking clean and trim.

I wish to note, also, that any measurements given here are for the

7

full-sized Minature Poodle and must be altered correspondingly for the smaller and larger-sized dogs.

As far as possible I have avoided using technical language. The layman cannot be expected to acquire an intimate knowledge of the dog's anatomy or the technical nomenclature before undertaking the grooming of his dog. I have, therefore, tried to make the instructions as simple and intelligible as possible.

Mistakes are inevitable for the novice. It would be the rare exception, indeed, who did not commit errors. They are the price of learning. Fortunately, however, the loss is not irretrievable for we are dealing with hair, which will grow back. The next time the mistake can be corrected. Patience and practice are the roads to success in dog grooming.

Finally, long experience has taught me the wisdom of following the sequence of instruction step-by-step, and I suggest the reader carefully do the same.

In conclusion, I wish to express my appreciation to my students for the ideas and suggestions they gave me as this book was progressing. Many of these have been incorporated into this book. The largest demand was for as many pictures and illustrations as possible. I have tried to provide these in abundance. By the same token I have limited the text and let the photographs and diagrams do most of the talking.

My thanks, especially, to Jane F. Kamp for joining me in this effort.

Dedicated to my daughter
Wendy Rose
and her Misty

Wendy and Misty

Contents

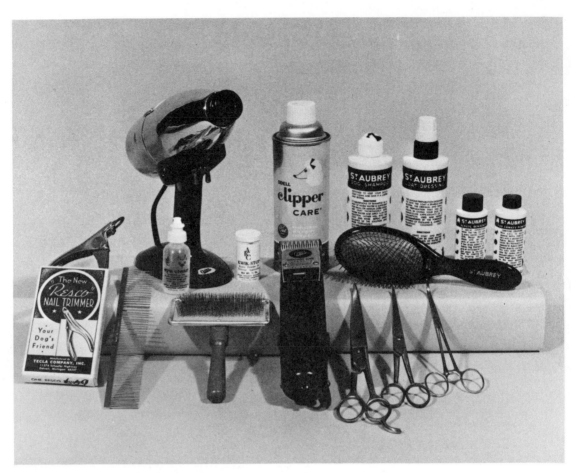

Photo 3. Essentials of grooming equipment

CHAPTER 1

Essentials of Grooming Equipment

DO NOT SKIMP on the quality of your tools. The less costly, inferior products in the long run can prove more expensive. The tool of better quality may cost a little more, but it will do a better job and last twice as long.

Be sure to have:

1. "Oster" clipper, Models A-2 or A-5 with blades No. 5, 10, 15, and 5/8. (John Oster Mfg. Co., Milwaukee, Wis.)
2. "Oster airjet dryer (same as above).
3. "Odell" clipper care (The Odell Company, Newark, New Jersey).
4. "Warner" dog-grooming brush (Warner Products, Baldwinsville, New York).
5. "Resco" nail trimmer (Tecla Company, Detroit, Michigan).
6. A Steel Comb, half-fine and half-coarse teeth.
7. Two pairs of barber scissors, one straight, one curved.
8. Shampoo, Ear Powder, Benzyl Benzoate, Coat Dressing, Pin Brush #100. (St. Aubrey Assoc. Inc., New York City).

There is no need to go into the detailed merits of the above-mentioned items, with the exception of the Oster clippers and the St. Aubrey line of accessories.

The Oster clippers, Models A-2 and A-5 are the best dog grooming clippers in the world. The Model A-5 has a detachable blade innovation, which gives greater speed in changing blades.

13

As for the St. Aubrey line, these products deserve special mention. The shampoo is super concentrated and rich in the essential oils. The ear canker powder aids in cleaning the ears and keeping them free from infection. The benzyl benzoate, when added to the shampoo, counteracts dry skin and protects against parasites. The coat dressing is a unique grooming preparation used in the finishing work. It aids the coat, imparts a sparkle to it, and leaves a lustrous finish. The St. Aubrey brush #100 is precision built to take care of the best show coats. The entire St. Aubrey line is the finest in the dog grooming field.

Photo 4. Before

Photo 5. After

CHAPTER 2

Brushing

CONTRARY TO POPULAR BELIEF, a dog *should not* be bathed before he is brushed. His coat should be freed completely of all tangles and mats before soaking it with water. The reason for this seems obvious. A matted coat will become more matted after the dog has been immersed in water and, therefore, doubly hard to brush out.

The Poodle or any long-haired dog for that matter, should be brushed regularly three or four times a week. When brushing is done systematically, only a minimum amount of time is required to brush out the dog before his bath. At the same time, this kind of regular brushing eliminates any discomfort the dog suffers from a matted coat.

In brushing (or in any phase of grooming your pet) it is best to start at the dog's hindquarters. This prevents the dog from seeing what is being done, thus giving him less reason to object. In addition, he becomes more easily accustomed to the grooming process. As a safeguard, before beginning, place a rubber mat under the dog to keep him from slipping or sliding.

Begin by brushing the left rear leg first, moving upwards and then downwards in short, fast strokes (*see* Photos 6 and 7). Brush thoroughly up and then down, and be sure to get beneath the surface coat. Feel for any mats or tangles with your hand and/or run a comb through the dog's hair. If his coat is free of tangles, proceed to the right rear leg and repeat the process. Then brush the two front legs.

Once the legs have been thoroughly brushed, start on the body coat, working from back to rear and making sure to brush underneath the body as well.

Head and ears come next. A part of the great beauty of the Poodle lies in his topknot and long, full ears. Spend a little extra time on both of these areas with brush and comb. Be particular about the pompon of the tail too.

Do not underestimate the importance of a thorough brushing. It, together with proper bathing, is the foundation of good grooming. A grooming job cannot possibly be very good, if the dog has not been properly brushed and bathed.

Conversely, any dog can be made to look good if he is brushed and bathed regularly. This is more than half the battle, although the word "battle" is used figuratively. For grooming should be a pleasure for both pet and owner. Part of this can be assured if you work systematically, and don't look for shortcuts or magic formulas, which my experience showed me only results in making the grooming more difficult.

Be sure the brush you purchase is a good one, with a foam backing and wire bristles that are not too sharp. The Warner slicker is perfect if it is available in your area. An inferior brush may look the same, but it will not do the same job. In places where the Warner brush is not in stock, ask your dealer to order one for you or write directly to the manufacturer.

Photo 6.   Brushing hindquarters

Photo 7.   Brushing topknot

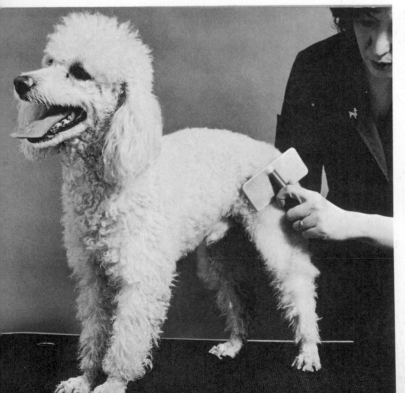

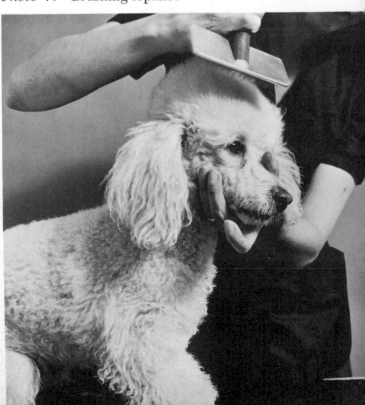

CHAPTER 3

Bathing

TO KEEP YOUR DOG LOOKING CLEAN and free of any odors, he should be bathed at least once a month. White dogs, of course, may require more frequent attention. At my dog-grooming school, I teach bathing the dog at the time of its monthly grooming since the monthly bath is usually sufficient and it is an essential part of the grooming process.

Prepare your materials before putting the dog in the tub. You will need a shampoo, a bristle brush, a sponge, and a towel. Have everything ready (*see* Photo 8).

If you decide to use a concentrated shampoo, dilute it first in a dish, then saturate the sponge with it. Attach a hose (purchasable at any hardware or variety store) to the faucet, to facilitate soaking

Photo 8. Bathing materials

Photo 9. Soaking

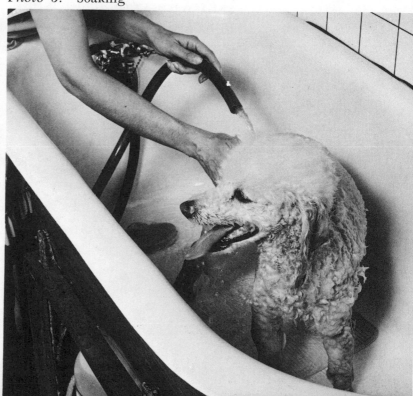

Photo 10. Sponging   *Photo 11.* Brushing lather

and rinsing the dog. The water should be warm, but not hot, and should always run free, never filling the tub.

Soak the dog thoroughly, starting at the rear, and working forward (*see* Photo 9). Pay particular attention to the rectum. Remember, too, that the Poodle's hair has a wool-like quality and is somewhat water resistant, so you will have to force the water through to his skin with your hand while you are soaking him. Be careful of the eyes and ears. Turn the ear flap (technically known as the fringes) over and hold your thumb against the ear canal when you wet the dog's ears, front and back. It's best not to put cotton in his ears. Placing the thumb against the ear canal is sufficient to keep the water out.

Since the dog will not be choosy about the moment he decides to shake the excess water from his coat and give you a bath too, it's a good idea to wear a plastic apron.

Once the dog has been soaked completely, take the sponge pre-saturated with shampoo and begin working up a good lather, again moving from back to front, and again paying attention to the rectum

18

Photo 12. Rinsing

Photo 13. Toweling

and the pads (bottom of the paws). Don't be stingy with the soap (*see* Photo 10).

Special care should be taken when washing the dog's head so that no soap gets into his eyes. A dog will never have the proper attitude toward his bath if it becomes a torturous experience, complete with burning eyes. Use your hands rather than the sponge in this area. There are also some "no tear" shampoos on the market, made especially for babies, which might be preferable for novices.

The next step is to take the small natural bristle brush and brush the lather into all parts of the body. Do not use a circular motion (*see* Photo 11). Then rinse the dog off from rear to front and be especially careful of the eyes and ears. Continue rinsing until all traces of soap have been washed away (*see* Photo 12).

Squeeze legs, ears, tail, and all parts of the dog's body gently with your hands to free him of excess water. Then rub him briskly with the towel (*see* Photo 13). Next, place the dog in an enclosed area and continue the drying with a blower. Do not allow the dog to dry completely, however. Leave the hair damp-dry.

CHAPTER 4

Fluff Drying

THE SECRET OF THE "POWDER PUFF" LOOK is in the fluff-drying process. Fluff drying is a combination of brushing and drying, with a blower. Hot air is directed at the area being brushed. A good dryer for this purpose is the one mentioned in the equipment section (see page 13), the Oster airjet dryer. (It can also be used in milady's boudoir if purchased with a hood.) Brush drying or fluff drying, as it is called in the trade, must be done systematically and methodically, starting with the legs, and moving on to the body, tail, head, and ears. Use *light* strokes, fluffing the dog's coat as the blowing process separates the hairs. (*see* Photo 14). Then quickly comb out the entire coat. When this is finished, rest the dog, and incidentally, yourself.

Actually, the brushing, bathing, and fluff-drying processes are considered the tedious part of grooming by some, although many pet lovers do not seem to mind this work in the least. When we realize that show dogs, with their tremendous coats, have to be brushed out for considerably longer periods, what we have done so far seems easy. Also, when one becomes adept in these techniques, the processes become simpler and go faster. It may be a cliché, but it is as true here as elsewhere: Practice makes perfect.

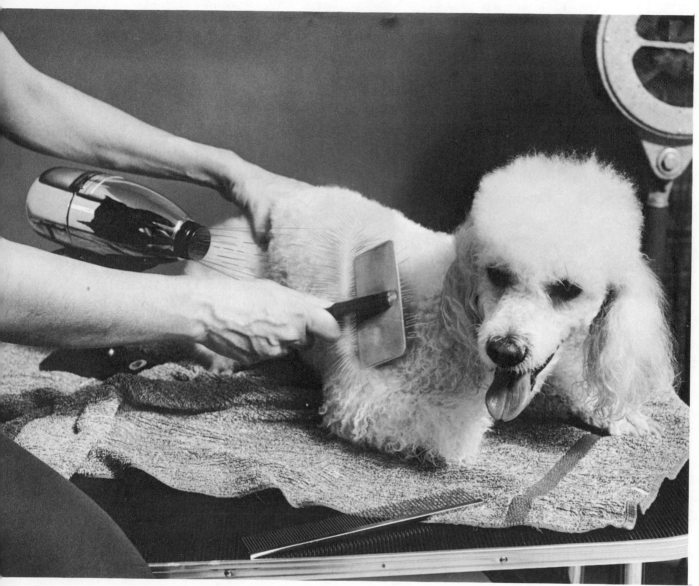

Photo 14. Fluff drying with Oster airjet

CHAPTER 5

Handling and Control

A BEGINNER WILL FIND IT AWKWARD at first to maneuver both dog and clippers at the same time. This is due principally to the fact that most of us are right-handed and few of us are ambidextrous. One of the first things, then, to be mastered in learning to clip a dog properly is the use of both hands. Almost every one of the author's students thinks this is impossible when the course begins. But by the end of the course, all are equally surprised that they had even questioned their ability to do so. In your first attempts at clipping, practice using your left hand if you are right-handed and your right hand if you are left-handed. Continue that way until the use of your other hand becomes automatic.

Another factor that accounts for a good deal of clumsiness in manipulating the dog to groom him is lack of control over the animal. An obedient dog is a prerequisite to good grooming, and this requires a handler who is firm and serious. Firmness does not mean roughness or brutality, but the dog must know who is the master and that his grooming period is not a time for play or petting. Our motto in dog handling is: "Firmness plus gentleness."

Think in terms of training a child. With a youngster we can be both firm in our demands and gentle in our manner of enforcing them. While this may not be the perfect analogy, there are enough similarities to suggest like methods. Of course, the owner of a spoiled dog has one advantage over the parents of a spoiled child. The dog in need of special correction can be referred to a dog-obedience trainer. For the spoiled child, we can offer only sympathy.

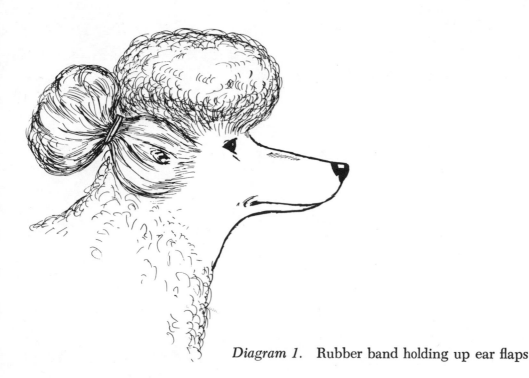

Diagram 1. Rubber band holding up ear flaps

The average dog, especially the Poodle, accustomed as it is to being groomed from puppyhood on, should not present a problem, unless the handler is not firm enough and the dog senses it. In those unusual cases where the dog is extremely spoiled or previously has been mistreated, it may prove impossible to do a good grooming job. Sometimes a specially constructed grooming sling may be used to control a balky dog.

One way to increase your control over the dog is to make certain that both you as groomer and the animal as subject are comfortable. If either is uncomfortable in any part of the grooming process, the dog is not being handled properly. A good deal of common sense must enter into this relationship. For example, there are logical points in each stage of the grooming process where the dog can sit or even lie down. Whenever this is possible, let him do so. But he must also stand when standing is required and stay when he is commanded to do so. Another area where a sensible approach is important is in the simple use of a rubber band to keep the ear flaps up while you are clipping or scissoring his front areas. But be careful not to have it on too tight. (*See* Diagram 1.)

CHAPTER 6

The Basic Clip

THE "BASIC CLIP" INCLUDES brushing, bathing and fluff drying, plus clipping of the face, feet and tail. *All other clips,* including the show clips, are based on this.

The BASIC CLIP, besides being the clipping foundation for all clips, is also all that is done on puppies from the tender age of six weeks to the time when a puppy's coat is profuse enough for straggly ends to appear. This usually becomes most obvious between three and four months, and the BASIC CLIP is all that is used. Afterwards, the puppy is put into the PUPPY-CLIP class, and there he remains until his coat has sufficiently matured to require one of the adult patterns.

On all clips, the No. 15 blade, a good general utility blade, is used for the face, feet, and tail. Memorize it in that order, 15, face, feet and tail, so that you won't forget either the blade or the procedure. When you are ready, attach your blade and begin.

Face

First, place the clipper at the center of the ear and clip in a single, direct, stroke to the corner of the eye. To accomplish this the ear flap will, of course, have to be held back with your other hand as Photograph 15 clearly illustrates.

Next, move the clippers back to your starting point at the ear and clip from one stroke lower on the face to the corner of the mouth. Now clip around the mouth. Hold the lips taut as you do this. (This will be the only time during the clipping process that the skin will be stretched.) Then do the other side of the face (see

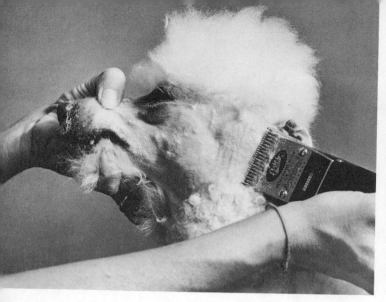

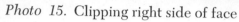

Photo 15. Clipping right side of face   Photo 15A. Clipping left side of face

Photo 15A) and under the throat but no lower than just below the Adam's apple. *Do not* clip the neck; this will be done later with the rest of the body. To complete the clipping of the face, place the clippers flat directly at eye level, and run them straight down the muzzle. Whatever hair remains *under* the eye or on the face is removed by working the clippers away from, but never toward, the eyes. Never clip *above* the eyes. (Note technique in Photos 16 and 17.)

Photo 16. Clipping under throat   Photo 17. Clipping down muzzle

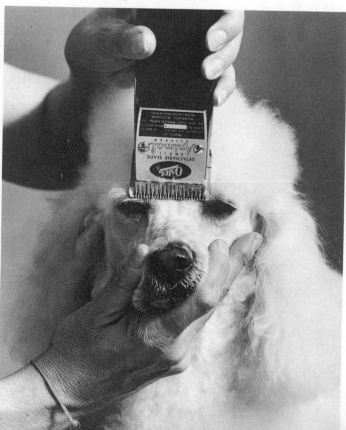

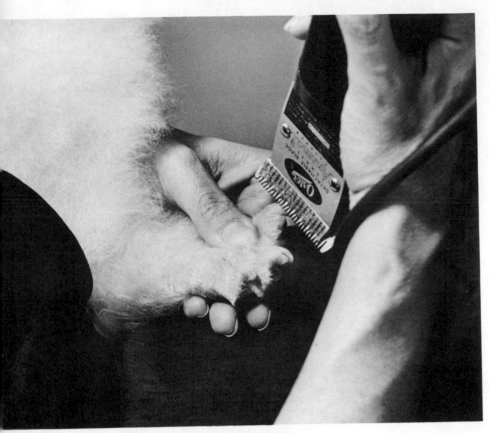

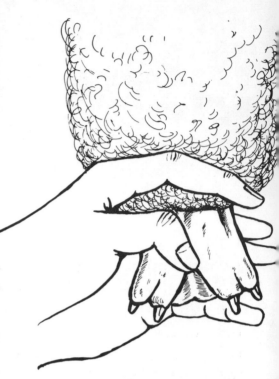

Photo 18. Clipping front of paw

Diagram 2. Press down to open paw

Feet

The feet or paws are probably the most difficult parts to do because the Poodle is most sensitive here, and the areas to be clipped aren't very wide, especially in the case of the Toy Poodle. Once one is proficient in clipping the paws, everything else is easy. The procedure you use is important, so start automatically with the rear paws, and before turning on the clippers, complete a silent run with them over the paw to be done. This will accustom both you and the dog to what is about to happen. When you are ready, turn the clipper on, and run it across the paw without taking any hair off, this time to accustom the dog to the sound. Work slowly and carefully as you clip off the excess hair covering the paw, and do not point the blade directly into the skin. Rather glide it along the flat of its back.

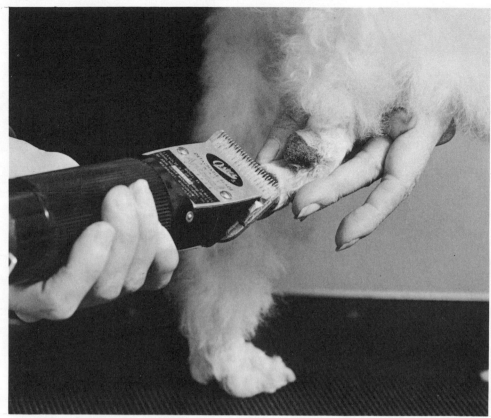

Photo 19. Clipping back of paw

Take hair off the paw up to the ankle. The most common mistake made in clipping the dog's legs is to go too high up on the ankle, so that the effect is one of the dog growing out of its pantaloons. When all the excess hair up to the ankle has been removed, the insides of the toes should be visible, and the hair between the toes can now be removed. Hold and spread the toes with one hand (*see* Photo 18 and Diagram 2) while you clip with the other. Use a side-to-side stroke, and take the utmost care not to dig into the web, which joins the toes. This is a sensitive membrane and easily cut. Then do the back of the paw (*see* Photo 19). To prevent any injury or pain to the dog, try to develop a light hand with the clippers. Of course, it is senseless to expect perfection with the first clipping, so don't try to remove every hair where continued probing will endanger the dog. Perfection will come with practice.

Photo 20. Clipping front of tail   *Photo 21.* Clipping back of tail

Tail

The length of the individual tail determines the amount to be clipped (*see* Photos 20, 21, and Diagram 3). If the tail has been docked correctly, it should be clipped approximately one and a half inches (for Miniatures), measuring from the rectum to the top. Some authorities in the dog world prefer that the tail be clipped a

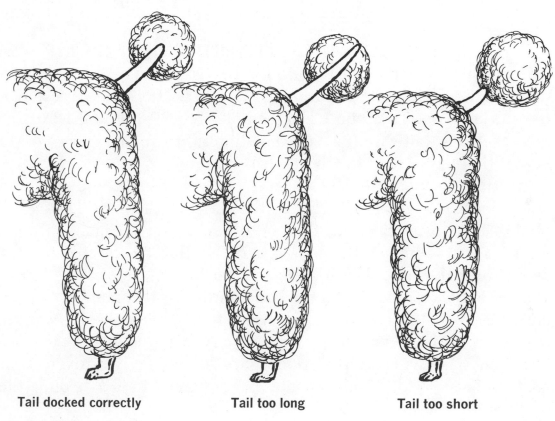

Tail docked correctly   **Tail too long**   **Tail too short**

Diagram 3.   Tail docking

longer length from the rectum, but I recommend the shorter clip and a full pompon. In my opinion, this enhances the beauty of the Poodle. However, if the tail has not been docked correctly and is longer than normal, it will have to be clipped in proportion to its length. Always try for the big pom.

Never clip into the rectum or any part of the rectum at any time.

CHAPTER 7

The Lamb Clip

THE "LAMB CLIP" RANKS WITH THE "DUTCH CLIP" (explained in Chapter 8) in popularity and is gaining more favor all the time because of its beauty and simplicity. It is the easiest pattern to keep up. To attain it, we complete the BASIC CLIP of the face, feet, and tail with the No. 15 blade, and then change to a No. 5 blade, the main blade for the LAMB pattern.

Starting at the base of the skull (*see* Photos 22 and 23) and going *with the grain*, we clip to the base of the tail. The No. 5 blade can clip no closer to the body than a half an inch, so don't worry about clipping the hair too close. But be careful to stay away from the legs. The legs should be full and clearly outlined. We are only concerned with the body outline at this point. We have clipped down the center of the back, from the base of the skull to the base of the tail, using the spine as a guide line. (*Also see* Diagram 4.) This should be done with long, steady strokes. Your next strokes on the body should be designed to leave only the outlines of the full legs.

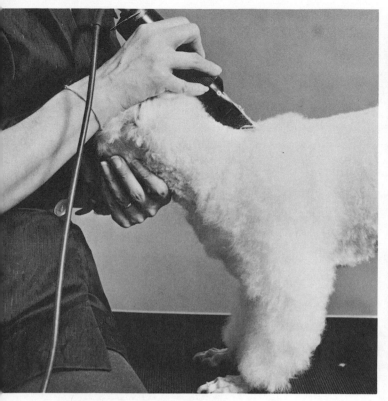

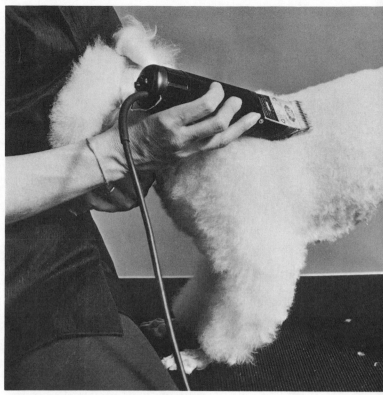

Photo 22. Starting the pattern

Photo 23. Continuing the pattern

Diagram 4. First step on lamb clip

31

Clip the sides of the body and continue underneath the body (*see* Photo 24 and Diagrams 5–7), taking particular care not to clip into the legs. Hold the dog up straight, grasping his two front legs in one hand, to clip the undersection. Run the clipper down the entire length of whatever coat is underneath. Do not worry about injuring the nipples, since the blade is flat and will glide right over them. In fact, it is important that the blade be flat on its back at all times, no matter what part of the body is being clipped.

For standard Poodles, who may prove too big and heavy to raise up, lift their legs one at a time to cut the hair underneath. The process is slower, but there is no alternative. Once the underbody is done, begin work on the neck.

The guide line for the neck is roughly from the Adam's apple to the collar bone in the front or from the bottom of the ear to the shoulder bone on the side. Clip the neck uniformly all around with the No. 5 blade since the closeness of the neck must correspond with the closeness of the body.

The legs and chest are left untouched until we get to the shaping and blending steps. Up to this point we have not considered the chest as a part of the body coat since it is preferable to leave this area a little fuller than the back, sides, and undersection.

Photo 24. Clipping the undersection

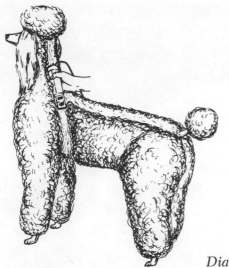

Diagram 5. Second step

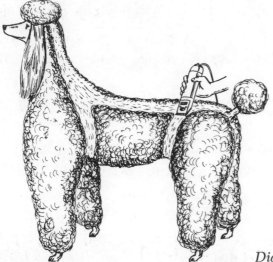

Diagram 6. Third step

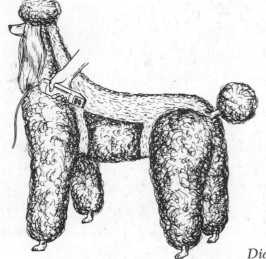

Diagram 7. Fourth step

33

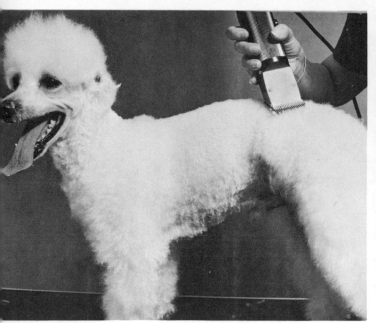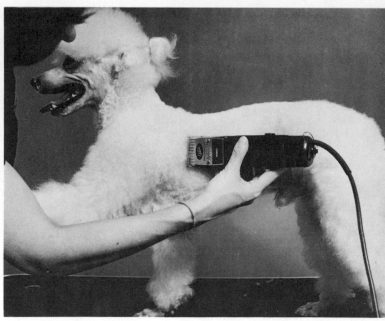

Photo 25. Shaping the rear leg   *Photo* 26. Shaping the front leg

Shaping and Blending

Blades No. 5 or No. 7 are used to shape and blend the body coat into the leg coat. But before you begin the clip, take up the comb and comb out the hair on the legs. Comb up and out, or if you prefer, out and up, the object being to have the hair standing straight out and away from the skin. A little practice may be necessary to master the proper wrist motion and achieve the desired results.

Once the combing is done, take up the clippers (is your No. 5 blade on?) and, starting at the very top of the leg coat, clip off *edges only* with the object of eliminating any line of demarcation between body and leg. It should be an imperceptible gradation with a graceful shaping and blending stroke with the clippers (*see* Photos 25 and 26).

How much hair is taken off the leg itself depends on whether you like full legs or closely trimmed legs. The author prefers the full leg. But common sense and personal preference will determine this. In any case, try not to dig, delve, or chop the fur. The blending technique requires a very light, graceful stroke, and it will take some time to perfect.

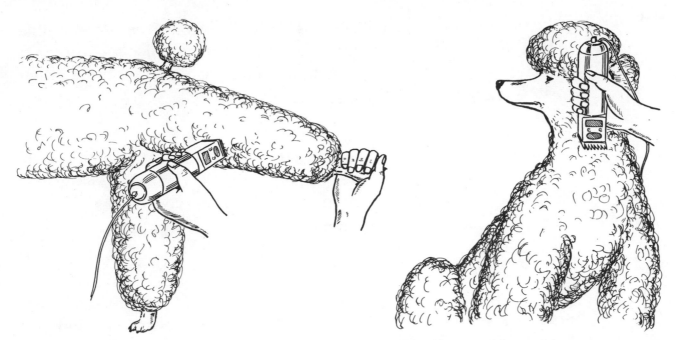

Diagram 8. Shaping legs

Diagram 9. Shaping front area

Since we are merely shaping the leg coat so that there is a gradual blending from body to leg, the clipper at this point is doing a lot of the scissors work. Keep in mind that it's always possibel to take off more hair, but never possible to put it back. Stay on the outside of the coat. It would be much better to err on the side of fullness, rather than to cut too closely.

Continue blending and shaping until you have achieved a nice, even, uniform line from top of leg coat to ankle. (*See* Diagram 8.) Do not be concerned if the ankle part does not blend perfectly with the rest of the leg. Such imperfection is left for correction and finishing by scissoring.

Some dog-grooming authorities believe that every part of the whole coat, including the legs, should be scissored. The author does not quarrel with them. In my opinion the technique we have worked out, of shaping and blending with the No. 5 blade, makes it more practical for the "do-it-yourself" poodle owner as well as the professional dog groomer and used as we have described here can cut the trimming time considerably. (*See* Diagram 9.)

If the novice feels that more time is needed in order to perfect this shaping and blending technique with the clippers, then recourse can always be made to the scissors. This will be more comprehensible in the following section on Scissoring. Meanwhile, we can best illustrate our point by saying that the clippers are simply another form of scissoring, only faster.

Scissoring

For both safety and satisfaction, it is best to invest in a good pair of scissors. I prefer the German-made shears, with fairly long blades, one pair with straight blades and one with curved blades.

Before starting the scissoring process, spray the entire coat first with St. Aubrey's Coat Dressing. As indicated in Chapter 1, this dressing will give the coat a lustrous finish and leave a pleasant fragrance.

Spray the dressing (holding the can about a foot away) onto the entire coat. First brush and then comb the spray into coat until fairly dry. Then proceed with scissoring.

Use the point where you stopped clipping on the ankle as a guide line. Brush down and scissor across in a sharp straight line. (*See* Photo 27). Now take the brush again, but this time brush upward and shake the dog's leg a little. This slight shaking motion causes the hair to puff out, so that when you pick up the leg and hold it out away from the body, you can observe the silhouette of the whole leg and scissor all stray edges (*see* Photo 28). First scissor the area around the ankle joint, then the rest of the leg (*see* Photo 29). Avoid snipping; follow the contours of the leg.

Do all four legs in the same fashion, stepping back occasionally to gain some perspective as to how the legs compare. They should be even and uniform. One can, of course, scissor indefinitely to achieve perfection, but you are not creating a masterpiece or modeling in clay. Do the legs look good? Good enough, then! You'll get better and better with practice.

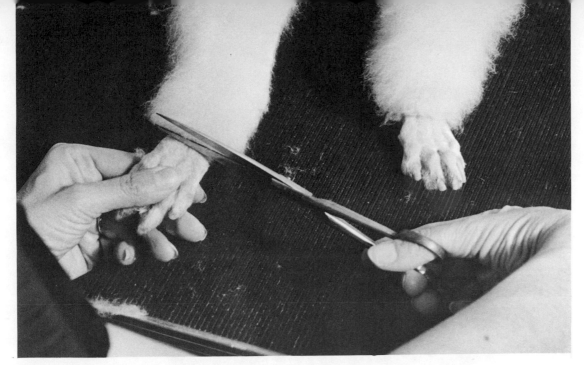

Photo 27. Scissoring the ankle

Photo 28. Scissoring the leg silhouette

Photo 29. Finish scissoring legs

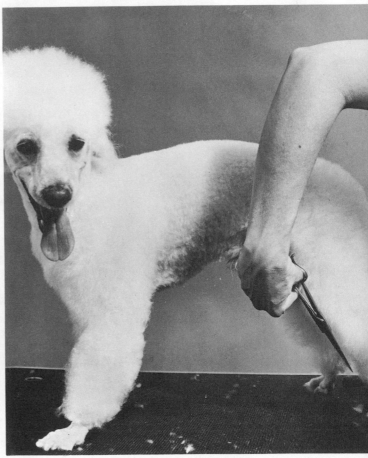

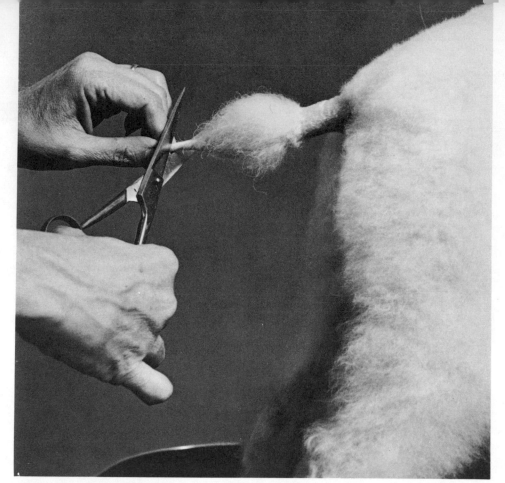

Photo 30. Scissor tail tip

Photo 31. Scissor tail pom

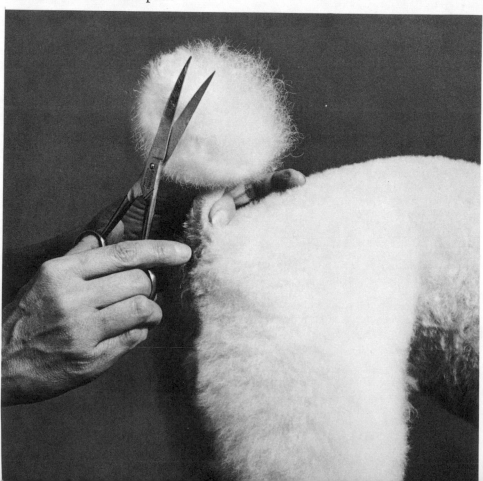

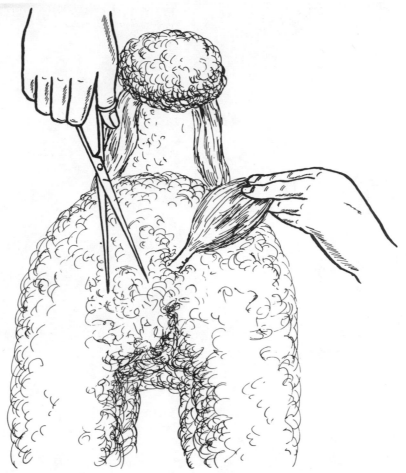

Diagram 10. Scissoring rectal area

To achieve a full "pom" effect, use the following technique in scissoring the tail:

Carefully twist the hair of the tail (not the tail itself) as tightly as possible in your hands. Once this is done, scissor the tip of the tail coat straight across (Photo 30). Then take a comb and comb out the pom. Stray edges then may be scissored with curved shears with the aim of giving the tail tip a round-ball effect or pom, as in Photograph 31. Now is the time, too, to scissor stray hairs in the rectal area (*see* Diagram 10) which, you will recall, we never clip. A full pom on the tail makes the Poodle a "thing of beauty and a joy from behind."

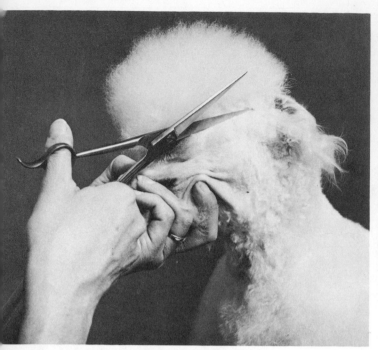

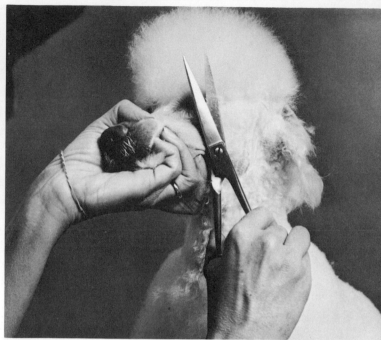

Photo 32. Start of scissoring topknot

Photo 33. Scissoring right side of topknot

Photo 34. Scissoring left side of topknot

Photo 35. Finish scissoring left side of topknot

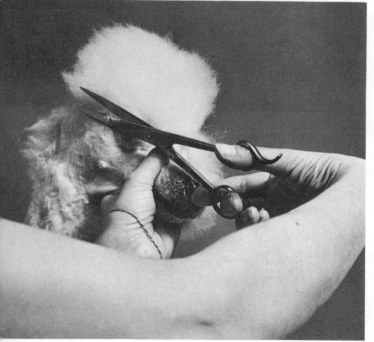

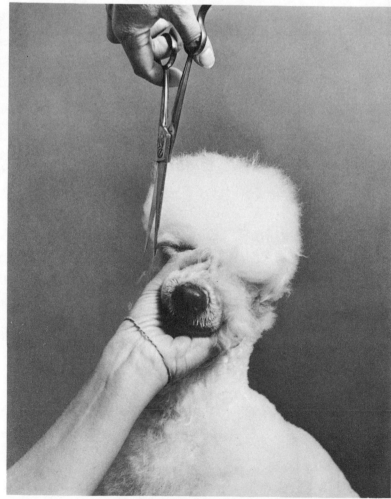

Photo 36. Lamb clip finished

The last main area for scissoring is the head, or more precisely, the topknot. This is done by using the facial conformation as a guide and cutting along the sides of the topknot. The top may then be done simply by scissoring it in proportion to the sides. Scissor evenly all around the topknot. (Photos 32–35 show the process step by step.) Stop when you're ahead, that is, when it looks good. Here again we leave perfection to the more practiced artisans.

Once legs, tail, and topknot have been scissored, pause a moment to get some feeling about the over-all effect. Do any of the legs need a little extra scissoring? Should the paws or the face be cleaned up just a bit more? Do whatever seems absolutely necessary, always taking care to use the correct blade in the correct manner. If everything looks good (as in Photo 36), you have finished the LAMB CLIP.

CHAPTER 8

Dutch Clip

WITH THE EXCEPTION OF THE SHOW CLIPS, the DUTCH CLIP is the most difficult to execute on a Poodle. The pattern is more complex and, therefore, requires more skill. In addition, it looks best on a dog whose body coat is thick and full. It will not look very well when the coat is fine or sparse. For dogs whose body coats are less than full, stick to the LAMB CLIP. It looks well on all dogs and is the easiest and cleanest clip to maintain.

One advantage of the DUTCH CLIP, besides its beauty, is that it can make a less-than-perfect dog look shorter or longer or whatever is required to give him the proper square look. The well-bred poodle is born with the square conformation. No camouflage should be necessary.

With all clips, the basic grooming procedure is the same, as we have indicated before. Brushing, bathing, fluff drying, and the clipping of the face, feet and tail, must be accomplished before you can proceed.

For the DUTCH CLIP use the No. 15 blade for the neck. We do the neck in the same fashion as we did in the LAMB CLIP, except that in the DUTCH CLIP we work against the grain. The DUTCH CLIP is the *only* clip where we clip against the grain. All other clips are with the grain. Our guide line for the neck is from the base of the ear to the shoulder bone on the side, or we continue down from the face to the collar bone in the front. The starting face-position is approximately two inches below the Adam's apple. The distance from the base of the topknot to the nape of the neck should measure about three inches. If you proceed in this fashion in back, front, and sides of neck, it will be evenly and uniformly clipped. (*See* Photo 37).

A variation done on the back of the neck is called the "V neck,"

Photo 37. Clipping the neck on the Dutch clip

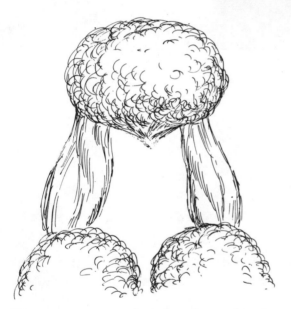

Diagram 11. V neck and traditional neck

which, as its name implies, is clipped at an acute angle to form the V. Note the two rear views of the dog in Diagram 11.

Now you can begin the pattern. Consult Diagram 12 to familiarize yourself with the way the DUTCH CLIP should look when completed. You will note that the pattern resembles a cross. The

43

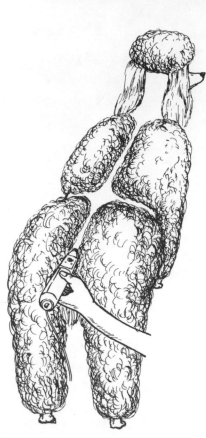

Diagram 12. Making the stripes on the Dutch clip

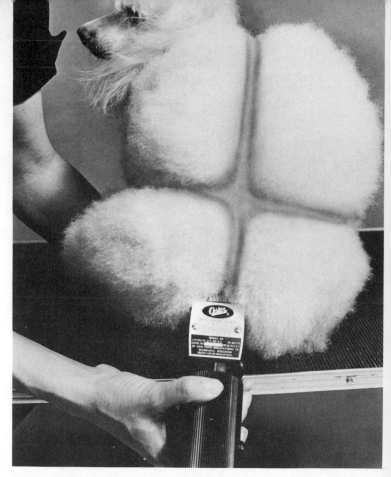

Photo 38. Starting the Dutch stripe

Photo 39. Clipping band around body

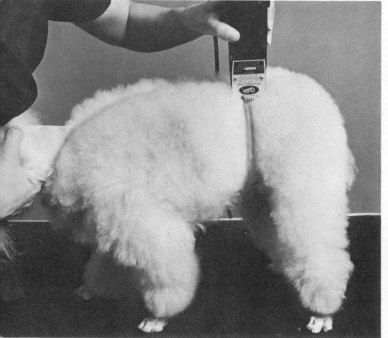

Photo 40. Finishing the vertical line

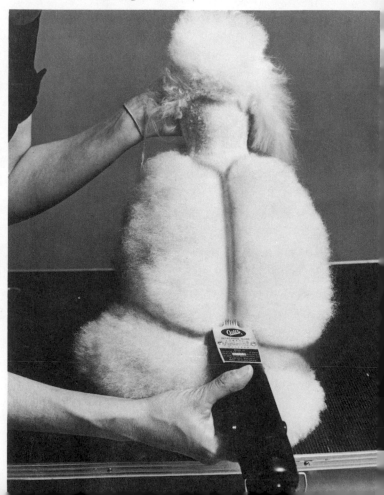

narrow line running from the nape of the neck to the base of the tail is clipped with a new blade made especially (by the Oster people) for this purpose: the 5/8-Poodle blade, or the Dutch blade. Before this blade came on the market, making the narrow stripe was a tedious process, but now it can be done quickly and easily.

With the Dutch blade attached to the clipper, and using the spine as a guide, place the blade at the base of the tail and clip a straight line up the center of the dog's back to the nape of his neck, moving *against* the grain. (*See* Photo 38.)

At this point it should be noted that the manner in which the dog is controlled while making this stripe is all important. If the dog moves suddenly or is permitted to stand in a crooked position, the result may well be a zigzag line, rather than a straight one. To protect oneself against such an uncomely error, it is best for the novice not to attempt to clip the stripe in a single stroke. Instead, the strokes can be broken up as follows: First, hold the dog upright by placing one hand under his stomach. Then clip the stripe—from the base of the tail up the spine to the point roughly to the last rib. Stop. Now start down the side adjacent to the leg and go down to the animal's stomach. (Photo 39.) Do the same thing on the other side. Now place your free hand under the dog's throat to hold him steady, and complete the stripe up the spine ending at the nape of the neck (as in Photo 40).

On a Toy or small Miniature Poodle, the width of the 5/8 blade itself determines the width of the stripe or band. On the larger Poodles, the No. 15 blade may be used for the stripe as the width of this blade will be in proportion to the size of the dog.

Any remaining hairs inside these bands can be cleaned up by placing the clippers (with the No. 15 blade) within the bands and slowly and carefully going over the narrow surfaces you have just clipped. Take particular care to line up the clippers properly with the edges of the bands before proceeding. Now you will note that at the very center of the pattern, where the stripes cross, the corners seem far too rigid and square in appearance. Clip the points diagonally, just enough to erase the square-edged look and to give a rounded effect. Do the same where the stripe ends at the neck. Of course, care must be taken to make these diagonals uniform. When all this is accomplished, we have the DUTCH CLIP pattern.

This pattern, resembling a cross, divides the body coat into four parts. The next step is to shape and blend these four parts into the four legs. Do each part slowly at first; speed will come later, and use the No. 5 blade.

Shaping and blending and the scissoring techniques are basically the same for every clip. For the proper procedure, see these sections under LAMB CLIP. There is one exception to the above. Whereas in the LAMB CLIP we clipped the edges off the top of the leg coat, we do not take the edges off on the DUTCH CLIP. At the conclusion of any clip, stand back, take a look, check your results with the diagrams and photographs in the book, and correct anything that requires correction. As has been mentioned, remember that the DUTCH CLIP is one of the more difficult clips, so it will take more time to perfect.

Big Poodles, the Caniche and Standard, and Poodles whose coats are fine and wispy or sparse, never seem to look good in the DUTCH CLIP. This particular clip seems to suit only the smaller-sized Poodles. However, for big-dog owners who prefer this type of cut, the ROYAL DUTCH CLIP, a variation of the DUTCH CLIP, exists, and the author prefers it. Actually the ROYAL DUTCH is the original DUTCH CLIP. The pattern we know by that name today came much later. The only difference between these two styles is in the width of the stripes. How much wider the one is than the other depends on personal preference.

Done properly the ROYAL DUTCH can be very becoming, but in the author's opinion, the TOWN and COUNTRY CLIP (Chapter 9) is the most attractive for the large Poodles.

CHAPTER 9

Town and Country Clip

The "TOWN AND COUNTRY CLIP" differs little from the LAMB CLIP. A No. 10 blade is used on the body, instead of a No. 5; the coat in the shoulder area is left high, clearly delineated from the body, and free of clipping about the edges; and an obvious separation between body and leg exists. Otherwise, the two are markedly similar and will present similar problems to the neophyte groomer.

Diagram 13. Town and Country

The No. 10 blade is used because it permits a closer trim than the No. 5 blade, leaving a quarter-inch coat instead of the No. 5's half inch. This shorter crop gives a nice, sleek look to the long-bodied dog. (*See* Diagram 13.) For the cold weather, a No. 7 blade might be used in place of the No. 10.

As the name of the clip suggests, it is the best for out-of-doors or country living, where the Standard Poodle seems most at home. He has long been noted as a wonderful hunting companion, and is probably the best in disposition, temperament, intelligence, and beauty of any breed in the dog world. The latter is, of course, a personal observation of the author's, but while it's not intended as a challenge to the lovers of other breeds, it should add some weight to the statement that this clip, properly executed, will accentuate all of the Standard's wonderful qualities.

CHAPTER 10

Summer Clip

THIS IS A WARM-WEATHER CLIP, obviously designed to decrease the dog's discomforts during the torrid days from July to late September. It calls for a close clipping of the entire body coat with either a No. 15 blade, or a No. 10 if the No. 15 seems to cut too close. (The No. 10 leaves a quarter-inch coat. *See* Diagram 14.) The author prefers the No. 10 blade for this Clip. The legs, too,

Diagram 14. Summer clip

are clipped, using the same blade as the one used for the body. Bracelets, however, are left full and later are scissored into round pompons (*See* Diagram 19.) The topknot, ears and tail also remain full. These parts naturally are never clipped but are scissored—preferably with curved scissors.

CHAPTER 11

Puppy Clip

WHEN THE PET POODLE IS STILL A PUP and his coat is not yet coarse, the PUPPY CLIP is used.

During this period, he will probably look more like a ball of fur than a Poodle to you, and his body coat, up to the age of nine or twelve months, will be too fine to be put into a mature pattern. But it will be long enough to require scissoring.

As stated in Chapter 5 on the BASIC CLIP, the pup's face, feet and tail should be clipped with the No. 15 blade, and straggly edges on the body coat and the pom of the tail, and the topknot should then be scissored. The amount of scissoring you do depends on how profuse a coat you desire, (*See* Diagram 15.) A certain

Diagram 15. Puppy clip for pet

amount of experimentation is in order here, particularly with a young dog.

It's well to note at this point that all handling and control problems during grooming are considerably minimized if your pup is accustomed to the process as soon as he is weaned—about six weeks. Then by the time the puppy is a few months old, your problems of controlling him while he is being groomed will be over. The old saw—a dog should not be groomed until he is six months or older—has no scientific basis whatever and, if followed, can considerably increase the amount of sweating and straining you must do to get your pet into the proper grooming habit.

Photo 41. The Puppy clip for the show ring. Jane Kamp, handler

CHAPTER 12

The Show Clips

THE "LION CLIP," as its name implies, makes the Poodle look like a lion, but with one difference. He will be a well-groomed, elegant, immaculate-looking lion. While this clip is common in England, it is rarely shown in the United States, so we will confine ourselves to describing the technique necessary to attain its first cousins: the ENGLISH SADDLE and CONTINENTAL CLIPS. Both of these are the accepted show clips in this country.

The English Saddle
Probably the most popular clip used in the American show ring is the ENGLISH SADDLE CLIP. It resembles the LION CLIP in every respect except for a "kidney patch" on both sides of the back. The entire back area then is made to look like a saddle, hence its name.

Like all other clips, the ENGLISH SADDLE begins with the BASIC CLIP of face, feet and tail, with one or two qualifications. An inverted "V" (Λ) is formed in the area above the eyes, but not accentuated to the point of looking odd, and no clipping at all is done on the dog's ankles. Instead the hair on the poms is permitted to slightly overlap the paw.

Naturally, the ENGLISH SADDLE, like other show clips, requires that the dog be endowed with a profuse coat. At least a four-inch length is necessary; five inches is even better. The best time to start grooming a dog for show is at four months, for it will take another six to ten months for the coat to attain its full growth. Meanwhile, he can be kept in the traditional PUPPY CLIP and trained for Puppy Class shows.

If he's to grow a good show coat, the puppy must be bathed once a week or once every two weeks, toweled and brushed dry, then fluffed out after the bath.

Some dog owners may question whether or not such frequent bathing is good for the puppy's coat and skin. The answer is that it is—*provided* the natural oils are restored, first, by using a shampoo with a lanolin base and then, by applying a good oil solution to the skin and coat. A number of these are on the market. The St. Aubrey line is an excellent one.

Now comes the technical part!

Hindquarters, or "Pack"

Assuming then, that the BASIC CLIP has been completed, take the scissors and trim a line completely around the body, at the mid-section, making sure to cut the back coat no shorter than two inches. This line will divide the mane from the hindquarters, and its starting point should be just behind the last rib (*see* Diagram 16).

Once this is done scissor everything below the dividing line along the hindquarters, moving continually against the grain and leaving approximately two inches on the entire back, or "pack," and two inches on the sides and legs.

Kidney Patch

The "kidney patch" is crescent or a half-moon shaped, but make it a small half-moon. Its constant shrinking in size is one of the variations which have taken place in the show ring over the past few years. The previous years it was much larger. Actually there is no precise measurement for it. It should be clipped and shaped in proportion to the dog's size and conformation. (*See* Diagram 17.)

Bracelets

The most intricate part of the show clip is shaping the leg bracelets, or pompons. Use Diagram 18 as a guide and starting with the rear legs, scissor a band on the stifle joint from Point A to B. Then cut another band just above the hock bone from Point C to D. Note how this band slants slightly downward. After these lines have been worked with the scissors, take the clippers, either the No. 15 or 30 blade, and go over the same areas again to assure that the bands

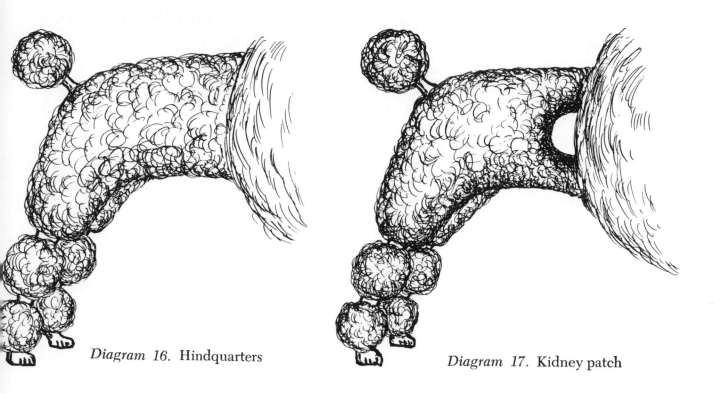

Diagram 16. Hindquarters

Diagram 17. Kidney patch

Diagram 18. Anatomy

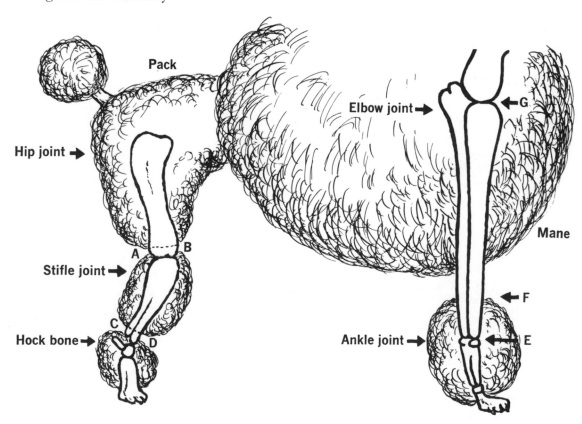

Pack

Elbow joint ➜

◄ G

Hip joint ➜

Mane

A   B

Stifle joint ➜

◄ F

C

Hock bone ➜   D

Ankle joint ➜   ◄ E

separating the bracelets are no more than one quarter of an inch wide and that they are clean. (This applies to Miniatures and Standards. On Toys it is only necessary to scissor the tops). Clip these bands with a short upward stroke.

Before cutting the bracelets on the front legs, using your hand only, feel along the dog's leg until you find the ankle joint (Point E). Use this to guide you in cutting the front leg bracelets. Everything above the bracelets should be trimmed up to the elbow joint where the leg joins the body (Point F to G). The bracelet itself should then be trimmed so that it is uniform. Half should be above the ankle joint and the balance should run right down to the paw, leaving no ankle exposed. In trimming the bracelet the object is to get as much of a round-ball effect as possible. Diagram 19 illustrates the method used to achieve this pom.

Mane

Half the knack of learning how to trim the mane lies in learning how to brush the heavy coat properly. Brush the mane forward, always brushing vigorously and against the grain, keeping a straight

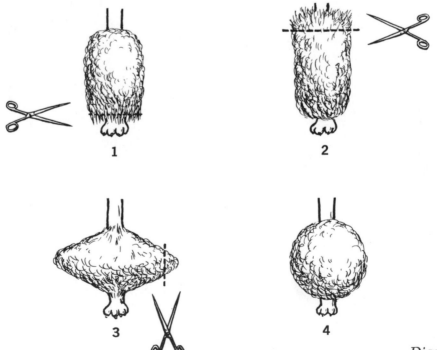

Diagram 19. Bracelets

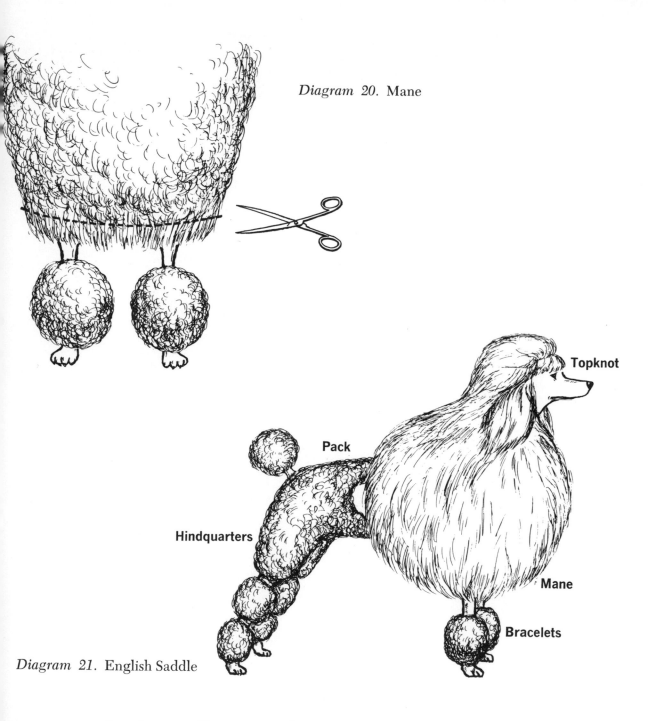

Diagram 20. Mane

Diagram 21. English Saddle

Topknot

Pack

Hindquarters

Mane

Bracelets

part to the skin at all times and separating the mane from the pack. A special brush for show coats must be used; the St. Aubrey pin brush is one of the best. This brush has been constructed so that it will not break the long silky hairs of the mane. Once the mane is separated from the pack, comb it gently in a light, flipping manner and scissor the straggly ends of the mane until you have achieved a rounded-muff effect. (*See* Diagrams 20 and 21.)

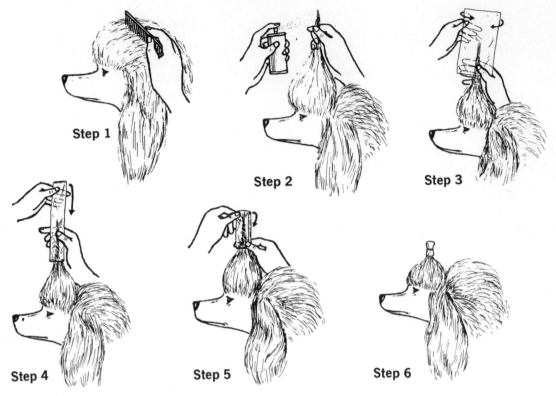

Diagram 22. Steps 1 to 6

Topknot and Ears

The long, flowing topknot and the long, low-hanging ears are probably the most noticeable and notable of all the best features of the show Poodle. And they require the most care and attention. They seem to be the parts most easily marred by split and broken hairs.

Actually creating the "Papillottes" for the show ring is no more than a simple process of good care and treatment for the topknot and ears.

Follow the steps outlined in Diagram 22. Begin by gathering the necessary materials: cut out four pieces of plastic material about three by five inches in size and have some small rubber bands on hand.

Step 1: Take the comb and separate the hair on the crown into two parts.

Step 2: Gather the front part in your hands and spray it with a coat conditioner.

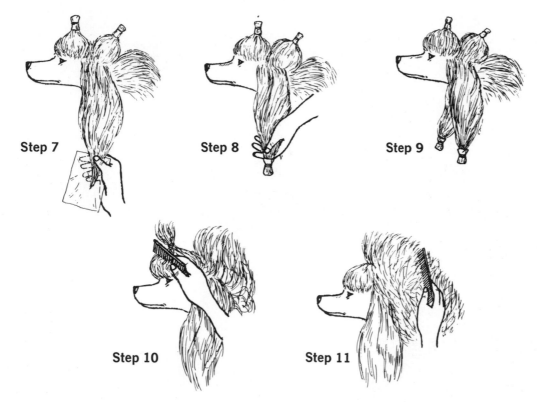

Step 7   Step 8   Step 9

Step 10   Step 11

Diagram 23. Steps 7 to 11

Steps 3, 4, and 5: Take one of the pieces of plastic and wrap it around the tips, then fold it over twice. Place cotton on the base of coat before the plastic is wrapped.

Step 6: Finally tie it with a small rubber band. The same procedure of course is followed for the back part of the crown.

Steps 7, 8 and 9: Handle the ears in the same manner, but be especially careful to see that the rubber band does not touch any part of the ear flap. In other words, only the hair should be banded, not the leather. This can be checked by running the comb through the ear tips where the leather ends.

Repeat the steps approximately every other day or about three times a week. On the day of the show, unwrap the papillottes, put a band around the front part of the crown, pulling it well back, and finish by combing the back part of the crown forward, producing a halo effect (Steps 10 and 11). The final touches come with combing and brushing down the ears, thus setting the face in the proper frame for the show ring. (*See* Diagram 23.)

Photo 42. The English Saddle. Jane Kamp, handler

The Continental Clip

Both the CONTINENTAL CLIP and ENGLISH SADDLE CLIP are done in the same way, except that in the former the hindquarter area is completely clipped (with the No. 15 or 30 blade) and just one set of bracelets on the rear ankles and pompons on the hips are left. The pompons, however, are optional.

Various ways can be improvised for obtaining the pompoms on the hip bone. Perhaps the simplest is to use an ordinary drinking glass as an outline and clip all of the hair outside the mouth. This establishes the pom shape so that you can freely clip the remainder of the hindquarters, except for the rear bracelets. Since the CONTINENTAL CLIP leaves no coat on the back or pack it becomes a much faster, easier clip than the ENGLISH SADDLE. (*see* Photo 43 and Diagram 24.)

Photo 43. The Continental clip

Diagram 24. Continental clip

61

CHAPTER 13

Other Clips

THERE ARE SEVERAL OTHER CLIPS, but they are all little more than variations of those already described. The SPORTING CLIP is very similar to the TOWN AND COUNTRY. The KENNEL CLIP is similar to the LAMB (except that you clip closer on the legs). There are also a few exotic clips, the inventions of dog owners who prefer to experiment and who want to try things that are a little different. But the clips illustrated in this book will provide the owner of a Poodle with all the variety he needs for practical purposes. In fact, the LAMB and DUTCH CLIPS account for some 90 percent of the most desired clips and the TOWN AND COUNTRY, PUPPY, and SUMMER CLIPS for the remaining 10 percent.

No two authorities will be in full agreement as to the exact manner in which a specific clip should be executed. The execution often depends upon the executioner. But in time, a groomer can develop his or her own style or evidence a flair for one or another cut which may become his trademark. A groomer has "arrived" when people stop and admire his work and persistently inquire who the groomer or grooming shop is who produced such a superb job.

For neophyte groomers, on the other hand, who simply wish to play safe with the least amount of fuss, the LAMB CLIP is best. Once the new groomer has mastered that and wants to be a little more fashionable, he can graduate to the DUTCH or ROYAL DUTCH CLIP. There is sufficient variety in the clips described in this book to satisfy most Poodle owners—including the most discriminating.

CHAPTER 14

Miscellaneous and Fine Points

LEARNING THE BASIC SKILLS is not enough for the Poodle owner who wants to have a professional looking job. Mastering the "fine points" of the art of dog grooming is also essential: Does the moustache look cute and suitable to the dog? Did you neglect to clean his ears or trim his nails? Is he completely clean? Have you avoided all clipper burns and rashes? Did you forget the bow and/or nail polish? Very often it is these extra little attentions that distinguish the exceptional groomer from an average one. If the groomer happens to be a professional, this distinction will prove its own reward by cementing the relationship between the customer and himself. Many Poodle owners will travel far out of their way to patronize a favorite groomer.

Moustache

To have a moustache or not have a moustache, that is the question—at least in the case of some Poodle owners. The author prefers a clean face, both for appearance and hygiene. Moustaches frequently become clogged with dirt and food, and cleaning them can be a constant chore. Still there are a substantial number of Poodle owners who desire them on their pets, and clipping them need not be difficult.

The simplest procedure is to clip from the eye halfway down the nose while you are working on the face, and leave the hair long around the entire muzzle for the moustache effect. Some people prefer the French moustache (*see* Diagram 25) because the under-jaw is clean and the moustache is chiefly on top with some of it

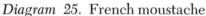

Diagram 25. French moustache   *Diagram 26.* Sweetheart moustache

falling slightly over the sides in a chic fashion.

The cutest of all is the Sweetheart moustache (*see* Diagram 26). This is shaped, as its name implies, like a heart and scissored short. The underside is clipped in proportion to the top.

Nails

City dogs are generally house pets, and in high-storied apartments where they make their homes they seldom get much exercise. Consquently, their nails do not receive the natural grinding, which comes with a reasonable amount of outdoor activity, and they have to be trimmed regularly. (See Diagram 27.)

The thing to be concerned about here is the quick under the nail. This is especially difficult to see on the black Poodle whose nails are also black. The beginning groomer should be content to trim just the tips at first. This is done by holding the paw firmly and trimming with short decisive strokes. (See Photo 44 and Diagram 27.)

When you become familiar with this operation, you will know exactly how high up on the nail to go without causing bleeding. But until you do, it is wise to play it safe, and if bleeding should

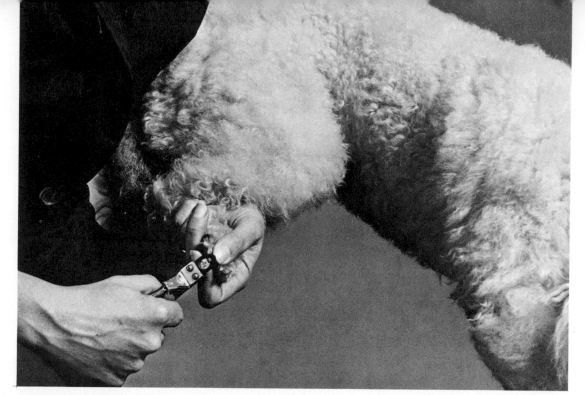

Photo 44. Trimming the nails

Diagram 27. Nail trimming

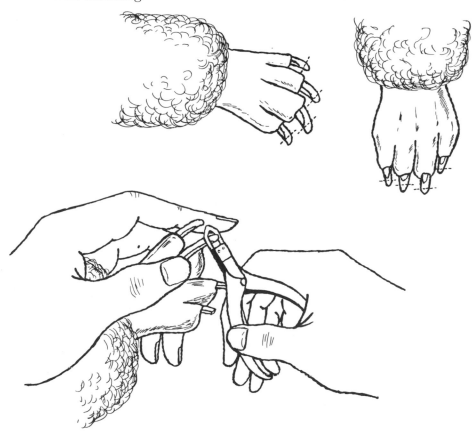

occur, have a can of ferric subsulfate on hand and dip the bleeding nail into the mixture. This stops the bleeding immediately. Ferric subsulfate is available at most drug stores in both powder and liquid form.

The best time to trim the dog's nails is just before the bath. The worst time (as many groomers have found to their sorrow) is at the end of the grooming job when the dog is a sparkling powder puff. If the nails are trimmed at this point and bleeding occurs, the coat may become smeared, and the job ruined. "For want of a nail . . ."

Nail Polish and Bows

Some finishing touches are not only a matter of the owner's whim, but also of geography. Polish and bows are more popular on the East Coast than the West Coast, and even throughout the East, opinion differs with region. What is common in one town may not be common in another.

If nail polish is used, however, select a good brand that will not come off the day after you put it on and a shade that complements the dog's coat coloring. Dogs do not like the smell of nail polish so it must be applied quickly.

To make the bow, cut approximately five inches off a yard of ribbon, then cut the remainder of the yard in half. Next cut the five-inch segment in half lengthwise.

Taking one of the longer pieces first, wrap it around two fingers. Slip it off your fingers and double it over. Now, cut off the corners

Diagram 28. Bow

66

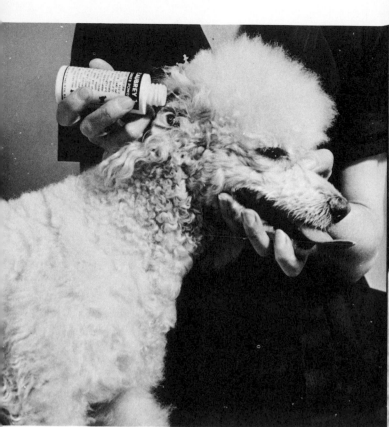

Photo 45. Shake powder into ear   *Photo 46.* Cleaning the ears

at the fold and "undouble" it. Tie the ribbon at the center, using the spliced segment. Once it is securely tied, separate each fold by gently pulling and twisting it out. Do both sides. Then use the excess of spliced ribbon to make a loop to fasten the bow to the dog. The loop may be slipped about a piece of hair and tightened (*see* Diagram 28). The dog may eventually shake it loose, but for a good while it will provide a nice ornament.

Ears

Purchase a can of Ear Canker powder (a St. Aubrey product) from your pet dealer, to help in cleaning your dog's ears. Shake a little of it into the ear, and spread it into the hairs. The powder will cause the hairs to become dry and brittle, and make it easier to pull out the hairs (*see* Photo 45). Use your fingers in the beginning; later when you are more experienced, a pair of hemostadts, or ear pluckers, may be used. (*See* Photo 46.)

Pluck the hairs with quick, decisive motions. The entire job should take only a few minutes.

The best time to clean the dog's ears is before the bath (at the same time that you trim his nails) so that any trace of the powder left on the coat will be washed away.

Never fool with the dog's ears if they are infected. This is a matter for the veterinarian.

Clipper Burns and Rashes

Many Poodle owners complain that their dogs come back from grooming salons with clipper burns and rashes. They state, as proof, either that the dog did not have anything like that before going to the grooming shop or that their veterinarians diagnosed the mark as a clipper burn.

To some extent this is true. There are times when the grooming salon is at fault. As a rule, however, this will not happen at a reputable grooming salon, where quality comes first. But dogs, like people, vary in skin sensitivity. Some have very tender skins and show such marks simply after a close clipping.

On those rare occasions when a clipper burn develops in spite of the best precautions, apply to the affected area one of a half-dozen soothing lotions that are specially prepared for dogs. In addition, try not to clip the sensitive spots as close the next time. If you would ordinarily use the No. 15 blade in these areas, use the No. 10.

Clipper burns may also develop if the clippers are allowed to run on so long that the blades get too hot. To avoid this, the groomer must feel the blade occasionally while clipping. A hot blade can be instantly cooled, lubricated, and sanitized with the Clipper Care spray. Before Clipper Care came on the market, the process took much longer. It was necessary to change the blades frequently or wait until the blade cooled down.

Clipping the dog before bathing him is still another cause of clipper rash. As the reader will recall, at the very beginning of this instruction, the necessity of thoroughly brushing and bathing the dog before clipping him was well stressed. The alternative can only lead to discomfort and perhaps infection from the combination of hot clippers on dirty skin. It is also much easier to clip a clean dog.

If, despite all precautions the dog shows undue irritation, have the veterinarian check him out.

Trimming the Stomach Area

In the male dog, excess hair along the penis must be clipped when the belly section is clipped. Use a No. 10 blade. It won't cut as close as the No. 15. Gently pull the penis down as you clip so that the hairs can be clearly seen and cleaned, and do not clip too close. (*See* Photo 47.) The excess hair on the testicles can then be carefully clipped with No. 10 blade.

Remember in clipping the female's undersection that there is no need to be concerned about the nipples. The clippers will glide right over them as long as you keep the blade lying flat on its back.

Incidentally, the author differs with those who believe that the

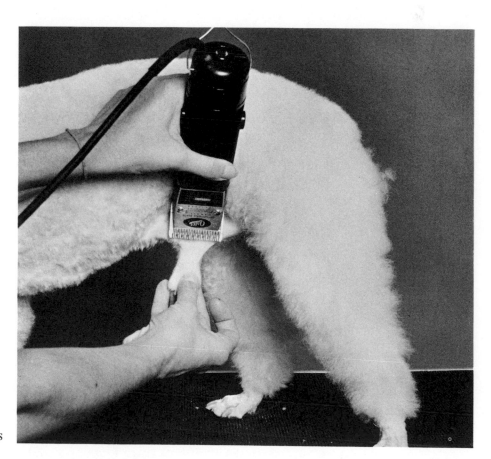

Photo 47. Cleaning privates

bitch should not be groomed during the latter part of her pregnancy. On the contrary, she can be made more comfortable by being properly groomed. This is, also, a time when the LAMB CLIP with its close, clean lines has some advantages over fuller clips.

Conditioning the Coat

The health of a dog and the condition of his coat are all important in grooming a dog, for one can build a superb superstructure only by first having a solid foundation. One of the laments of many dog owners, especially Poodle fanciers, is the deplorable condition of their dog's coat.

A great deal of this is due to the dog's diet, in addition to the extensive backyard breeding that goes on and, of course, creates inferior strains. If one is foolish enough to buy a dog from a less than reputable source, he's stuck with his purchase, and even if he thinks he's gotten a bargain, it may prove a costly error in the long run. Remember all puppies look good at eight weeks old, even when the breeder is not an expert.

For dry, flaky skin or a drab and lusterless coat, try feeding the dog bacon fat. It's especially good for itching, dandruff, and dry skin. If the dog is too thin and has a flaky coat, put him on a lamb diet for two or three months. It may work wonders. A good marrowbone is excellent to keep his teeth healthy.

As mentioned earlier, harsh shampoos always should be avoided. A good shampoo containing lanolin or cocoanut oil plus a good diet and frequent brushing is the surest formula for raising a healthy dog with a good coat.

Buying a Puppy

When buying a puppy, go only to a professional breeder whose reputation you know is good. It very often happens that the pup will cost less from the professional breeder than from the backyard pet owner. And even if the professional's price is considerably higher, buying from the non-professional is generally a poor alternative, if not an out and out waste of money.

How often we have heard the laments: "I was told it was going to be a Toy, and look at what I got—a Standard!" Or, "We were promised the papers, but we never got them." Or, "Why can't my dog look like the others I've seen?" The answer is simple. Most new dog owners know little about identifying or raising animals until they have their own pet. They even need the aid of a reliable breeder to properly identify their choice and to be sure that the pup they get is physically fit and has had the proper care and shots. In the case of Poodles, tails must also have been properly docked and dewclaws removed. In addition, it is of the utmost importance that the dog comes from the type of breeder who will accustom him to good grooming as soon as he is old enough. This will halve the chores of the new puppy owner who decides to do it himself.

Flea Baths

Fleas are not only a discomfort to your dog, but can be dangerous to his health. So don't waste any time in combating them once they appear. There are several good medicated shampoos on the market, that are simple to apply. Instead of using the regular shampoo for ordinary bathing, use a flea shampoo. It usually comes in concentrated form, works up a good lather, and may be used the same way as the regular shampoo is used.

Since the flea season lasts for a period of several months, generally from July to October, switch to a flea shampoo during this period as a preventive measure.

Tinting

Tinting or dyeing a dog to a particular color, is possible only with white or light-colored dogs, and should only be done with a vegetable dye that is easy to wash off. The method is simple enough:

Fill a large vessel or baby tub with about two gallons of water. Empty two capsules of the desired shade into the water and stir until the color is uniform throughout. Put this vessel aside until you give the dog his regular bath. Then, while he is still wet, pour the colored water over him with a pan or pot. Use your hands to spread the coloring through his coat, working it into all parts so that the new shade is even. Then towel him off and proceed with the rest of the grooming process.

Eye Stains

It will be noticed, on white or light colored dogs, that a deep dark stain forms under the eyes. Thus, at the end of the grooming job, if this is not attended to, we will have ugly stains on an otherwise beautiful dog.

These stains are caused by the tearing of the eyes which evidently have a strong acid element, resulting in discoloration. We then use a combination of an eye clear preparation to control the tearing and temporarily camouflage the stain by applying a color stick. We recommend for this purpose Stein's Lining Color Stick, put out by the M. Stein Co., N.Y.C.

Like Your Work

Taking care of a dog, especially the Poodle, is no lazy man's paradise. But not all of it is unpleasant or overly difficult. Many dog owners have become professionals, simply because they are so fond of animals. And of these, several hold top positions in the dog world.

Whether done by a professional or amateur, expert or beginner, however, the grooming process should be a pleasure, not an ordeal, for both dog and groomer. The ideal relationship is one where the dog looks forward to being groomed. What a happy advertisement it is for the dog-grooming salon when a patron's dog comes in wagging his tail instead of tugging at his leash. The whole process is easier when the dog is not balky or frightened, and the groomer can then do a more careful job.

CHAPTER 15

The Dog-Grooming Salon

THIS SECTION IS DEVOTED TO THOSE who wish to go beyond trimming their own dog or dogs, and who desire to turn this hobby into a profitable career. Proper schooling, while not required by law, is of course necessary. If you decide after some practice to turn professional, attend a school, and take a Shop Owner Course such as the one given by the New York School of Dog Grooming.

Three factors make such a choice attractive:

It permits you to support yourself and also to combine both avocation and vocation.

It is a growing and profitable field.

The investment needed is very low.

A major part of the investment will go into equipment. A professional groomer requires professional tools. The following is a list of the essentials.

1. Cages (preferably of galvanized metal or steel). (Photo 48.)
2. Cage dryer (for drying). (Photo 48.)
3. Floor dryer (for fluffing). (Photo 49.)
4. Bathtub. This can be a used model, but must stand or be elevated to a waist-high position. (See Photo 50.)
5. Grooming table with post and loop. (Photo 51.)
6. Clippers, blades, shampoos, brushes, combs, nail trimmers, scissors, ear powders, ear plucker, as well as all the necessary cleaning equipment. An important item here is a good vacuum cleaner. We recommend the Industrial Shop Vacuum which can be purchased at Sears Roebuck.

The popularity of the Poodle has become so great in recent years that it is no accident that dog-grooming salons are flourishing throughout the country and in the past few years have become an industry in themselves. Indeed, pets—whether it involves breeding them, caring for them, or grooming them—have become big business.

Of course, the field can be quite competitive, and selecting a location for your salon is as important in dog grooming as in any other business and must be done carefully. Where the field is already crowded, and there are many established salons, it is difficult for the newcomer to survive. However, there are still many areas where no shops exist or where competition is negligible and trade is available. A professional who takes pride in his work and is not exorbitant in his fees has nothing to fear.

Photo 48. Cage set up

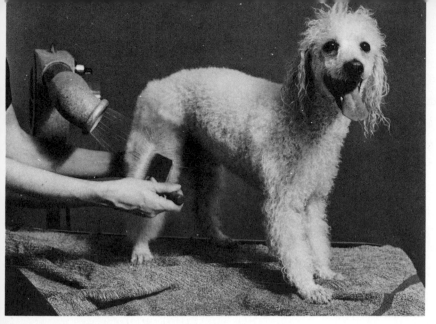

Photo 49. Fluff drying with professional dryer

Photo 50. Bathtub waist high

Photo 51. Professional work area

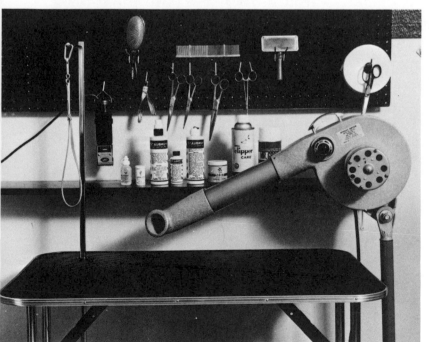

Setting Up a Shop

To insure the success of the new dog-grooming salon three things are necessary and in the following order:

1. Quality grooming
2. A desirable location
3. A good shop set-up

We have already discussed the first two factors. The third requires more elaboration. As to the decor, every effort should be made to make the shop as bright as possible. Good light aids grooming efficiency. For example, the walls should be painted a light color to brighten the grooming area, and the lighting fixtures should be selected on how much light they cast, and on their appearance. Strong daylight, of course, provides ideal lighting, but it is never enough, particularly during winter when darkness comes early and many days are overcast. The reception room can be done in any color, and, in general, personal preference can prevail.

Probably the most expensive single item that you will have to buy for the shop will be the cages. Each dog that comes into your shop should have a separate cage. These cages come either in units of two, four, six or eight, or they can be custom-made in singles (see Photo 48.) The best type of cages are made of galvanized metal or steel and are equipped with sliding pans for easy cleaning. Prices vary depending on quality and make. A unit of four will cost about $200.

Your next most expensive purchase will be the floor dryer used to damp dry and fluff dry the dog. These dryers run between $120 and $160. Most shops require two or more. You will also need grooming tables (of the Safari type), which come complete with a grooming post and cost about $42 each. Clippers, blades, scissors, combs, brushes, shampoos, nail trimmers, and other minor items. The total for these will probably come to about $200. (*See* Photo 51.)

Roughly, then, the entire cost of these essential items, will be in the neighborhood of $600. So you can realistically think, of opening a shop, including rent, fixtures, and furnishings, with a minimum capital of $1,000. Of course, you will need a reserve until the business is on a sound basis. Still assuming that the investment totals somewhere between $1,500 and $2,000, what other business exists where an individual can reap substantial returns within a year's time on such a low original investment?

Cleanliness is a necessity in a dog-grooming shop. You cannot overdo the cleaning, disinfecting, and sanitizing. The first impression made on a customer should be the best one, and a spotless shop is half the battle. This means a well-kept workroom, as well as reception room. The days of the "pet shop look," with foul odors and littered floors, are gone forever.

Another *must* is insurance. Two types are necessary: A property damage and public-liability policy and a plateglass policy. Both have low annual premiums.

Learn the prevailing price-scale in the salon's immediate and surrounding area before you set your fees and charge accordingly. Do not overcharge for a service nor start out with cut-rate prices in the hope of enticing customers away from a nearby competitor. You will find it extremely difficult to raise your prices later.

It is also well to educate your customers on the desirabilty of coming regularly—on an average of once a month or, at the most, every six weeks—to groom their dogs. Add an extra charge if the lapse of time is any greater. Also, charge extra if a dog is neglected and comes in badly matted, requiring considerable time for brushing. Flea baths also may warrant an extra fee. Such extra charges should not be exorbitant. If properly fixed, they may help to teach the owner to keep his dog in better condition by giving him the incentive to bring the animal in for regular grooming.

Hang diagrams or photographs of the various clips (Diagram 29) on your wall. (You might want to copy the drawings of clips in this book.) Be sure they are in a prominent spot so that the customer can point to it and say, "That's the clip I want." This saves a lot of confusion and aggravation. Also, have your scale of prices prominently displayed so that there is no mix-up or embarrassment regarding any of your fees.

Some advertising is essential. Get as much good publicity as you can. And always remember, the best recommendation is a satisfied customer.

Try to carry some accessories, such as brushes, combs, collars, leashes, coats, shampoos, and deodorants. This may provide an important convenience for your customers—and a supplement to your income.

Try your hand at breeding. Start with good stock. Selling puppies can prove an important source of income. Become an expert, if you can, on the fine points and faults of puppies. Such knowledge will pay off!

Diagram 29. Pick your clip

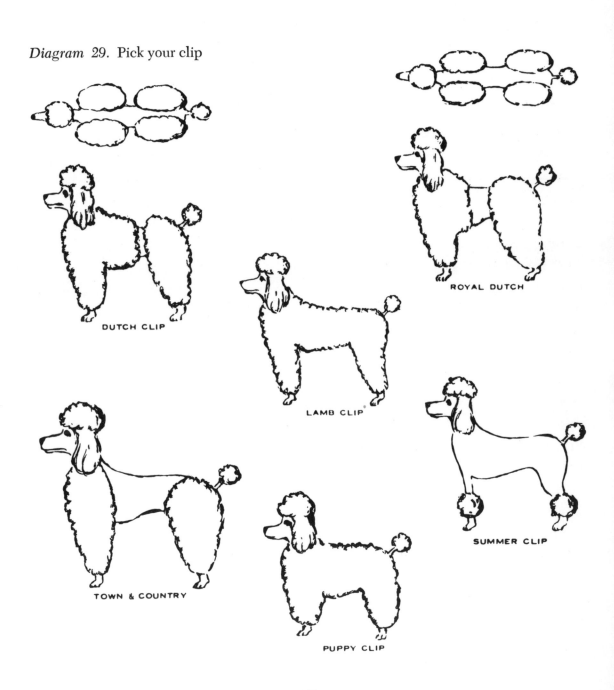

DUTCH CLIP

ROYAL DUTCH

LAMB CLIP

TOWN & COUNTRY

PUPPY CLIP

SUMMER CLIP

CHAPTER 16

Conclusion

REGARDLESS OF WHETHER THE STUDENT is just interested in "doing it himself," or turning a hobby into a profitable business, his primary goal should be to do the best possible job of grooming the dog.

For those who feel unsure about their aptitude for handling grooming on a professional basis, I say: "Take your time!" Move slowly before making any substantial investment. *Do not* invest in a shop of your own before you are absolutely confident of your own abilities. Because if you lack confidence, your customers won't have confidence in you either.

Don't try to fake a clip that you don't really know. Experimentation is for after hours and innovations should be tried on your own dog first—unless you tell the customer that there will be no charge. This time it's just for the sake of experience.

Read as much theory as you can and acquaint yourself with the different types of Poodles and their histories. Whether an individual Poodle owner or professional groomer, the more you know about these dogs, the better off you'll be. It's amazing how many questions will be thrown at you relating to your own dog or the Poodles with which you work.

How do you tell a good puppy from a poor one? What color is the best? How often should a bitch be mated? Where do we find a good stud? The answers to these and many more would be found in any comprehensive book on dogs.

Never attempt to substitute for a veterinarian. To each his own. A badly infected ear, a peculiar body growth, overcharged anal glands, or the hundred-and-one symptoms or diseases to which the dog is heir can be judged and treated properly only by the man who has been trained to treat them—the veterinarian.

On the other hand, some questions can be simply answerd on the basis of reading and study. If you don't know an answer say so. If you do, be as helpful, clear, and specific in your answer as possible. Don't use confusing big terms. If you are a professional, good advice will help in gaining the confidence of the customer, and will benefit you too. Proper care and feeding of animals means happy customers.

Your own dog, too, can be a walking advertisement for you. An improperly cared for, uncomfortable looking, unkempt, or over-pampered Poodle will never win you any friends or customers. On the other hand, the elegant beauty, striding gracefully alongside his master, is the most elequent testimonial to you as the owner, handler, and groomer.